The

#BookTalk
&

#BookGram
Fan's
Pocket Journal

The #BookTalk & #BookGram Fan's Pocket Journal
A Fill-In Book for Readers Who Live Between Pages and Posts

Part of The Fan's Pocket Journal Series

By Leaves of Gold Press
Edited by C. Egan

ISBN: 978-1-923212-53-4 (paperback)

Dewey Decimal Classification: 028.9
BISAC Subjects:
LITERARY CRITICISM / Books & Reading (LIT004120)
LANGUAGE ARTS & DISCIPLINES / Literacy (LAN009000)
SOCIAL SCIENCE / Media Studies (SOC052000)

Disclaimer: TikTok and Instagram are registered trademarks of their respective owners. This publication is not affiliated with, sponsored by, or endorsed by TikTok, ByteDance, Instagram, or Meta. All references to #Booktok and #Bookstagram are descriptive of reader communities and are used in an unofficial, editorial context.

Copyright (C) 2025 Leaves of Gold Press
ABN 67 099 575 078
PO Box 345, Shoreham, 3916, Victoria, Australia

THE #BOOKTALK & #BOOKGRAM FAN'S POCKET JOURNAL

Fill-In Book for Readers Who Live Between Pages and Posts

Part of The Fan's Pocket Journal Series

The Fan's Pocket Journal Series:

The Marginalia Fan's Pocket Journal

The Magic Academy Fan's Pocket Journal

The #BookTalk & #BookGram Fan's Pocket Journal

The Romantasy Fan's Pocket Journal

. . . and many more!

For every reader who ever said,
'#BookTok made me do it,' and every shelfie that made us
fall in love on #Bookstagram.

.

How to Use This Journal

This journal is made for readers who don't just read books—they live them, post about them, cry over them, and recommend them at 2 a.m.

Inside you'll find 30 prompts inspired by #BookTok and #Bookstagram: some for writing, some for doodling, some for colour swatches and shelf aesthetics. There's no wrong way to use them.

Skip around.

Fill it in while you're mid-binge-read or after a book haul.

Post your favourite spreads on TikTok, Instagram, or wherever your bookish friends gather.

Think of this as a content companion to your bookshelf, a mixture of memory-keeper, trend tracker, and creative playground.

Your reading life is already worth documenting. This journal just gives it the space.

CONTENTS

Chapter One:
My #BookTok or
#Bookstagram
Identity

My #BookTok or #Bookstagram Username

What's your current username, or your dream one? The one that captures your reader vibe.

My #BookTok or #Bookstagram name is:

_____

I chose this because…

_____

_____

_____

_____

_____

Sketch your profile pic or logo here.

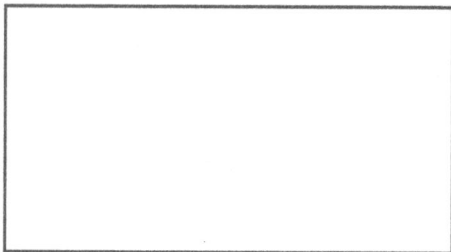

```
┌─────────────────────────────┐
│                             │
│                             │
│                             │
│                             │
│                             │
│                             │
└─────────────────────────────┘
```

Three Emojis That Sum Up My Reader Aesthetic

Your aesthetic in emoji form! Books, sparkles, coffee mugs, crying faces, swords, crowns, dragons… whatever feels like you.

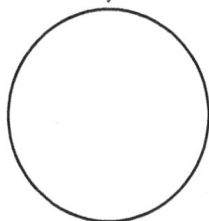 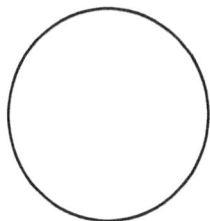 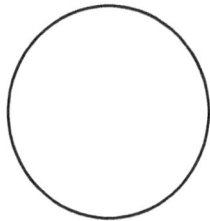

Emoji 1   Emoji 2   Emoji 3

Here's why I picked them…

_____

_____

_____

_____

_____

_____

Decorate this page in your aesthetic colours.

Share your reader tagline. #BookTok #Bookstagram #ReaderLife

My #BookTok or #Bookstagram Tagline

Imagine a slogan that sums up your reading identity. Short, bold, unforgettable.

Brainstorming ideas:

_____

_____

_____

_____

My tagline is: _____

Design or decorate your tagline visually:

CHAPTER TWO:
SHELF TALK

The Book I'd Feature First on My Shelf Tour

Imagine your camera is rolling. Which book do you grab first to show off, and why?

The first book I'd feature is: _____

_____

Because...

_____

_____

_____

_____

Sketch or decorate the book cover here.

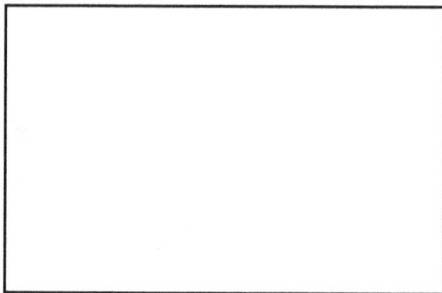

My Rainbow Shelf

Some arrange by spine colour, others by vibe. How would you build your rainbow shelf?

Fill or color these spines.

My rainbow shelf would be arranged by...

_____

_____

_____

The Book I Hide Behind Pretty Covers

Every reader has that one guilty-pleasure or messy-fave book. Write it down here, and tell us why the pretty cover saves it.

The book is: _____

I hide it because… _____

Design or paste the cover that hides the chaos.

Share your shelf vibe or emoji mix. #ShelfTalk #BookTok #Bookstagram

CHAPTER THREE:
TROPES I CRAVE

A Trope I'll Never Get Tired Of

Enemies to lovers? Found family? Grumpy x sunshine? Write the one trope that always hooks you.

My forever trope is: _____

I love it because...

_____

_____

_____

_____

_____

_____

Sketch or symbolise this trope (two crossed swords, linked hands, a crown, etc.).

The Most Unhinged Trope Combo I Secretly Love

Some tropes are chaotic together, but that's what makes them fun. Combine two or more here.

Trope A + Trope B = Chaos.

_____

_____

_____

_____

_____

_____

Illustrate or describe the chaos.

A Trope I'll Never Forgive an Author For Using

Which trope ruins a story for you? Drop it here and rant freely.

The unforgivable trope is…

_____

_____

_____

_____

_____

_____

Visualise your rage here!

Share your fave trope combo. #BookTokMadeMeReadIt #TropeTalk

CHAPTER FOUR:
VIRAL MOMENTS

The Book That Made Me Sob on Camera

Every BookTokker or Bookstagrammer has a breakdown book. Which one shattered you? Write it here.

The book was _____

What broke me: _____

_____

_____

_____

_____

_____

Tear stains, mascara smudges, or dramatic cover sketch. Draw it here.

My Top Plot Twist Moment

The twist that made you throw the book across **the room** (or whisper-shout "WHAT?!").

The twist was in _____

_____

_____

_____

Why it destroyed me...

_____

_____

_____

_____

_____

Draw your
shocked reaction
face here.

The Book I'd Risk Spoilers to Rant About

Some books are so intense, you can't stay quiet.
Which one makes you spill spoilers just to talk about it?

The book is: _____

My rant starts with... _____

_____

Sketch or write your spoiler rants here!

Share your wildest plot
twist reaction. #PlotTwist
#BookTok #BookReaction

CHAPTER FIVE:
WORLDS & WONDERS

My Dream Creature Companion

Is your dream companion a dragon, gryphon, robot, ghost, wolf, shadow beast, or something never seen before? Describe it here.

My companion is a _____

named _____

Personality, powers, quirks:

_____

_____

_____

_____

Sketch your companion here:

If I Had a Power or Gift

From magic to perfect recall, from invisibility to time travel—what ability would define you?

My power would be...

_____

_____

_____

_____

_____

_____

_____

Draw an emblem for this power.

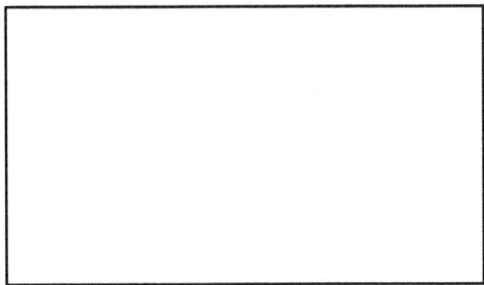

Share your dream companion sketch. #FantasyFans #BookstagramArt #BookTok

The Fictional World I'd Most Want to Live In

Choose a world from books, or imagine your own.
What makes it irresistible?

The world is called _____

It's known for... _____

Sketch your world's banner, map, or symbol.

Chapter Six:
Story Moments

My Favourite Meet Cute

A "meet cute" is a story moment where two characters first encounter each other in an unusual, charming, or memorable way. In romance, fantasy, or even thrillers, chance encounters shape the story. Which one made you grin the most?

The meet cute I love most is: _____

Because: _____

_____

_____

Sketch or symbolise the scene (coffee spill, sword clash, library stumble…).

Share your funniest annotated line. #AnnotationNation #BookTok #Bookstagram

The Cliffhanger That Broke Me ⌛

That ending where you had to grab the next book (or scream into the void). What was it?

The cliffhanger was in: _____

What it did to me: _____

_____

_____

_____

_____

_____

Draw your cliffhanger reaction here.

The Ending I Still Can't Stop Thinking About

Bittersweet, shocking, perfect, or infuriating, some endings never leave us. Which one stuck with you?

The ending of _____

. . . stays with me because... _____

_____

_____

_____

Illustrate it with a symbol or quote fragment.

CHAPTER SEVEN:
READER AESTHETICS

My Annotation Colour Palette

Highlighters, sticky tabs, fountain pens! Every annotator has a system. Swatch yours here.

Color 1

I use this color for: _____

Color 2

I use this color for: _____

Color 3

I use this color for: _____

Color 4

I use this color for: _____

My secret colour-coding rules.

_____

_____

_____

_____

My Favourite Bookshelf Cosy Vibe

What does your ideal reading space look like?

Candles, fairy lights, blankets, cats, dragons? Describe and doodle it here.

My vibe looks like...

_____

_____

_____

_____

_____

Sketch or decorate your cosy corner.

♫ If My Reading Nook Had a Theme Song

Every vibe has a soundtrack. What song matches your nook, and why?

The song is _____

by _____

Because... _____

Decorate this page with lyrics, doodles, or vibes.

Share your shelf vibe or palette. #Shelfie #BookTok #BookNook

Chapter Eight:
The Social Media Effect

The Last Book I Bought Because of Social Media

Social media made you do it. What was the book, and did it live up to the hype?

The book was _____

My reaction after reading: _____

_____

_____

_____

_____

Sketch the book haul moment.

Share your latest "BookTok made me buy it." #Book-TokMadeMeBuyIt #BookstagramRecs

The Unboxing of My Dreams

If you filmed an unboxing, what would be inside? Signed editions, sprayed edges, fan art, candles?

In my fantasy unboxing, I'd unwrap...

_____

_____

_____

_____

_____

_____

_____

Draw or list your dream items here.

The Most Overhyped Book I Secretly Loved (or Hated)

Some books blow up on #BookTok and #Bookstagram. Did you join the hype, or rebel against it?

The book was _____

My verdict: Loved / Hated / Mixed.

Hot take notes: _____

_____

_____

_____

_____

Doodle or decorate your verdict.

CHAPTER NINE:
MY BOOKISH COMMUNITY

The BookTokker or Bookstagrammer I'd Love to Buddy-Read With

If you could pick anyone on social media (or any reader-friend), who would it be, and what book would you read together?

I'd buddy-read with _____

The book we'd tackle is _____

Because _____

_____

_____

Draw your buddy-reading vibe (two stacks of books, a chat bubble, a couch…).

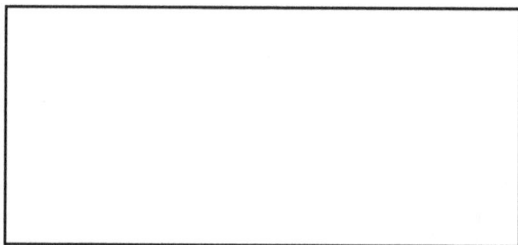

Share a tag with a reading buddy. #BookBesties #Bookstagram #BookTok

If I Hosted a Readathon

Readathons can have wild or cosy themes.
What would yours look like?

The theme of my readathon would be _____

_____

_____

_____

_____

_____

_____

Design your readathon logo or flyer.

The Comment or Reaction That Made My Day

What's the funniest, kindest, or most unhinged comment you've ever received—or left?

The comment was: _____

_____

_____

_____

_____

_____

Fill in with quotes, doodles, or fake comments—

Chapter Ten:
The Legacy of My Shelf

⏳ If Future Readers Found My Books...

Imagine someone inherits your shelf years from now. What will they learn about you?

They would say: _____

_____

Because my books show... _____

_____

_____

_____

_____

Draw a time capsule or shelf silhouette here.

Share your forever book rec. #BookRecs #BookTok #Bookstagram

The One Story I'll Always Recommend on #Bookstagram or #BookTok ☆

That book you'll never shut up about, the one everyone should read at least once.

The story is: _____

I recommend it because… _____

_____

_____

_____

Sketch a symbol for this story.

♡ My #Bookstagram or #BookTok Legacy

When people look back at my bookish social media era, what will I be known for?

They'll remember me as _____

_____

_____

_____

_____

Design your #BookTok or #Bookstagram crest, logo, or vibe statement here.

Notes Pages

"There is no friend as loyal as a book."
~ Ernest Hemingway

The Fan's Pocket Journal Series:

The Marginalia Fan's Pocket Journal

The Magic Academy Fan's Pocket Journal

The #BookTalk & #BookGram Fan's Pocket Journal

The Romantasy Fan's Pocket Journal

. . . and many more!

From #BookTok to #Bookstagram,
the magic is the same—stories shared.

Your fandom, your shelves, your story.

Fill these pages with the books that found you.

This space belongs to your bookish journey.

**YOUR VOICE CREATES
THE BOOKS YOU'LL
READ TOMORROW**

If this book brought you joy, please leave a review on Amazon, Goodreads, or your favourite online bookstore.

Reviews aren't just words, they're signals that help other readers discover these journals. Each review also directly supports the creation of more Fan's Pocket Journals, so your voice truly shapes what comes next!

For readers who crave worlds of wonder. . .

Enter a world of secrets, quests, and hidden love. Critically acclaimed The Bitterbynde Trilogy is the fantasy romance you'll never forget.

Secrets, quests, and love entwined

THE BITTERBYNDE TRILOGY

The fantasy romance critics acclaim

Available in all good bookstores

Readers who thrive on unforgettable stories will find The Bitterbynde Trilogy impossible to resist. Acclaimed by critics, it combines the lush worldbuilding of fantasy with the emotional depth of romance, pulling you into a landscape where secrets, quests, and hidden identities keep every page alive with discovery.

Its language is rich yet accessible, rewarding those who savor beautiful prose while still delivering a plot that drives forward.

For anyone who loves books that not only entertain but linger in the imagination, this trilogy is the kind you don't just read, you inhabit.

The Bitterbynde Trilogy
by Cecilia Dart-Thornton

Book #1 The Ill-Made Mute
Book #2 The Lady of the Sorrows
Book #3 The Battle of Evernight

www.ingramcontent.com/pod-product-compliance
Lightning Source LLC
LaVergne TN
LVHW011338080426
835513LV00006B/428